To a beautiful
Bride...

To a beautiful
Bride…

MARKS &
SPENCER

Marks and Spencer p.l.c.
Baker Street, London W1U 8EP
www.marksandspencer.com

Copyright © Exclusive Editions 2003

This book was created by Magpie Books,
an imprint of Constable & Robinson Ltd.

Designed by Tony and Penny Mills

A copy of the British Library Cataloguing-in-Publication
Data is available from the British Library

ISBN 1-84273-921-2

Printed in China

INTRODUCTION

The very thought of a wedding fills all our hearts with happiness and excitement. This is the bride's day; her mother will shed a tear, her father's chest will swell with pride but she will be the magnet that draws all eyes to her. For the rest of her life, this day will be her brightest memory.

This little collection of poems and thoughts has been put together in celebration of the beauty of brides through the ages and in honour of the love and devotion they have inspired. Although society has changed over the years, the hopes of the human heart have remained constant. In this book we raise a glass of champagne to the bride and wish her a perfect day.

When one finds a worthy wife, her value is far beyond pearls. Her husband, entrusting his heart to her, has an unfailing prize.

PROVERBS 31:10–11

Blest is the bride on whom the sun doth shine.

ROBERT HERRICK

(1591–1674)

Throw open the door; come forth, O bride.
See how the wedding-torches shake
Their heads, their fiery tresses flying free
To welcome you.
A shy young bride, half bashful,
Half excited; she hesitates
Until love's calling draws her on,
Melting in tears.
No tears today! No girl on earth
So beautiful; no girl will see
A fairer wedding-day than this
Dawn in the east.
The day is waiting.
Come forward, sweet, and hear our song;
Our torches dip their golden heads
To welcome you. This day is yours—

CATULLUS

(c. 60 BC)

My Dear Miss

I am a farmer in a small way and my age is rather more than forty years and my mother lives with me and keeps my house, and she has been very poorly lately and cannot stir about much and I think I should be more comfortabler with a wife.

I have had my eye on you for a long time and I think you are a very nice young woman and one that would make me happy if only you think so …

I have about 73 pund in Naisbro Bank and we have a nice little parlour downstairs with a blue carpet and an oven beside the fireplace and the old woman on the other side smoking … and you could sit all day in the easy chair and knit and mend my kytles and leggums, and you could make the tea ready agin I come in, and you could make butter for Pately Market, and I would drive you to church every Sunday in the spring cart and I would do all that bees in my power to make you happy. So I hope to hear from you. I am in desprit and Yurnest, and will marry you at May Day, or if my mother dies afore I shall want you afore. If only you will accept of me, my dear, we could be very happy together.

I hope you will let me know your mind by return of post, and if you are favourable I will come up to scratch. So no more at present from your well-wisher and true love—

Simon Fallowfield

P.S. I hope you will say nothing about this. If you will not accept of me I have another very nice woman in my eye, and I think I shall marry her if you do not accept of me, but I thought you would suit me mother better, she being very crusty at times.

The proposal was refused

When rice is thrown after a bride
it should be scattered by the
married and not by the
unmarried ladies present.
Manners and Rules of Good Society
(1912)

The best friend is likely to acquire
the best wife, because a good
marriage is based on the talent
for friendship.

FRIEDRICH NIETZSCHE

(1844–1900)

I...chose my wife, as she did her
wedding gown, not for a fine
glossy surface, but such qualities
as would wear well.

OLIVER GOLDSMITH

(1728–1774)

from *The Vicar of Wakefield*

TO MY BRIDE

To my bride, I give you my heart
Sharing love each day, from the very start
To my bride, I give you my kiss
Filling each day with joy and bliss
To my bride, I give you my being
To love, to play, to work and to sing
To my bride, I give you my mind
Learning each day to be more kind
To my bride, I give you my soul
Growing together to be more whole
To my bride, I give you my life
Rejoicing each day that you are my wife.

STEVEN REISER

With reference to the choice of horses for the occasion, at one time a pair of greys were considered indispensable for the bride's carriage . . . But that is now all changed, and it is thought better taste to have browns or bays. The fact is that a smart pair of greys has been found to attract much notice, with the consequence that an undesirable crowd frequently assembles at the bride's house. This gathering is mainly composed of nurses in charge of perambulators, butchers' boys . . . to say nothing of fishmongers' – , whose proximity is not always pleasant.

MRS HUMPHRY

from *Manners for Women*

(1897)

The trousseau consists, in this country, of all the habiliments necessary for a lady's use in the first two or three years of her married life; like every other outfit there are always a number of articles introduced into it that are next to useless, and are only calculated for the vainglory of the ostentatious.

The Habits of Good Society
(1859)

Roses are red, diddle diddle,
violets are blue,
If you'll have me, diddle
diddle, I will have you.
WOMEN'S LEAP-YEAR
TRADITIONAL BALLAD

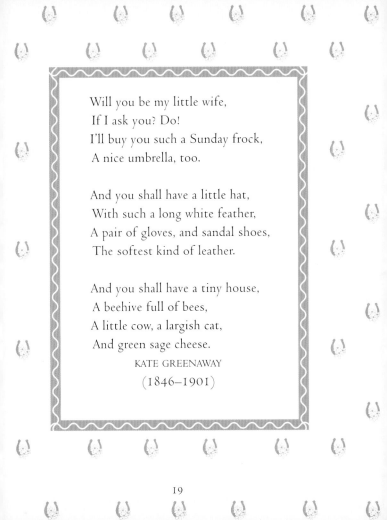

Will you be my little wife,
If I ask you? Do!
I'll buy you such a Sunday frock,
A nice umbrella, too.

And you shall have a little hat,
With such a long white feather,
A pair of gloves, and sandal shoes,
The softest kind of leather.

And you shall have a tiny house,
A beehive full of bees,
A little cow, a largish cat,
And green sage cheese.

KATE GREENAWAY

(1846–1901)

TO MY DEAR AND LOVING HUSBAND

If ever two were one, then surely we.
If ever man were lov'd by wife, then thee.
If ever wife was happy in a man,
Compare with me, ye women, if you can.
I prize thy love more than whole Mines
    of gold
Or all the riches that the East doth hold.
My love is such that Rivers cannot quench,
Nor ought but love from thee give
    recompense.
Thy love is such I can no way repay.
The heavens reward thee manifold, I pray.
Then while we live, in love let's so persever
That when we live no more, we may live ever.

ANNE BRADSTREET

(1612–1672)

The mayor's office being within a mile and a half of the farm, they made their way there on foot, and returned in the same manner after the church ceremony was over. At first the procession was compact, a single band of colour billowing across the fields, all along the narrow path that wound through the green corn; but soon it stretched and split up into groups, that dawdled to gossip. The fiddler led the way, his violin decorated with rosettes and ribbon streamers. After him came the bride and bridegroom, then the relatives, then the friends, in any order; and the children kept at the back, amusing themselves by plucking bell-flowers from among the oat stalks, or playing among themselves without being seen. Emma's dress was too long and dragged a little on the ground. Now and again she stopped to pull it up, and then with her gloved fingers she daintily removed the coarse

grasses and thistle burrs, while Charles waited,
empty handed, until she had finished.

GUSTAVE FLAUBERT

(1821–1880)

from *Madame Bovary*

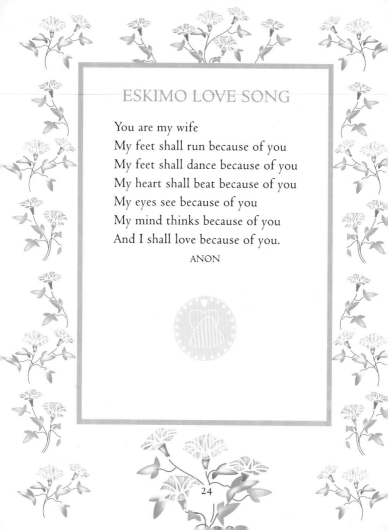

ESKIMO LOVE SONG

You are my wife
My feet shall run because of you
My feet shall dance because of you
My heart shall beat because of you
My eyes see because of you
My mind thinks because of you
And I shall love because of you.

ANON

Happy above all must be that marriage where neither husband nor wife ever had a friend so dear as one another.

DINAH MARIA MULOCK CRAIK

(1826–1887)

from *A Woman's Thoughts About Women*

The voice that breathed o'er Eden,
That earliest wedding day,
The primal marriage blessing,
It hath no passed away.

JOHN KEBLE
(1792–1866)
'Holy Matrimony' hymn

BLESSING OF THE APACHES

Now you will feel no rain, for each of you will be
shelter for the other.

Now you will feel no cold, for each of you will be
warmth to the other.

Now there will be no loneliness, for each of you will
be companion to the other.

Now you are two persons, but there is only one life
before you.

May beauty surround you both in the journey ahead
and through all the years.

May happiness be your companion and your days
together be good and long upon the earth.

ANON

A woman seldom asks advice
before she has bought her
wedding clothes.
JOSEPH ADDISON
(1672–1719)

Our respectful advice to the young ladies is, to seek for a young gentleman who unites in himself the best qualities of all, and the worst weaknesses of none, and to lead him forthwith to the hymeneal altar, whether he will or no.

CHARLES DICKENS

(1812–1870)

from *Sketches by Boz*

It is now held by many that the prudent and modest maiden should not even allow her lover (even after their engagement) to kiss her. Not until after marriage should such a favour be granted.

JULIA M. BAILEY

from *Modern Manners and Social Forms*

(1889)

ON

MARRIAGE

FROM THE PROPHET

Then Almitra spoke again and said, And what of Marriage, master?

And he answered saying:

You were born together, and together you shall be for evermore.

You shall be together when the white wings of death scatter your days.

Ay, you shall be together even in the silent memory of God.

But let there be spaces in your togetherness,

And let the winds of the heavens dance between you.

Love one another, but make not a bond of love:

Let it rather be a moving sea between the shores of your souls.

Fill each other's cup but drink not from one cup.

Give one another of your bread but eat not from the same loaf.

Sing and dance together and be joyous, but let each one of you be alone.

Even as the strings of a lute are alone though they quiver with the same music.

Give your hearts, but not into each other's keeping.
For only the hand of Life can contain your hearts.
And stand together yet not too near together:
For the pillars of the temple stand apart,
And the oak tree and the cypress grow not in each
  other's shadow.

KAHLIL GIBRAN

(1883–1931)

A successful marriage requires falling
in love many times, always with the
same person.
MIGNON MCLAUGHLIN
(B. 1915)

Love does not consist in gazing at each
other, but in looking outward together
in the same direction.
ANTOINE DE SAINT-EXUPERY
(1900–1944)

The Responsibilities of a
Bridegroom from a pecuniary
point of view commence from the
moment of his engagement.
Manners and Rules of Good Society
(1912)

There is only one happiness in life;
to love and be loved.

GEORGE SAND

(1804–1876)

I write to you from here [Windsor] the happiest, happiest Being that ever existed. Really, I do not think it possible for any one in the world to be happier, or as happy as I am. He is an Angel, and his kindness and affection for me is really touching. To look in those dear eyes, and that dear sunny face, is enough to make me adore him. What I can do to make him happy will be my greatest delight.

QUEEN VICTORIA
from a letter to King Leopold
written the day after her wedding
(1840)

THE GOOD-MORROW

I wonder by my troth, what thou and I
    Did, till we lov'd? Were we not wean'd till then,
But suck'd on country pleasures, childishly?
    Or snorted we in the seven sleepers' den?
'Twas so; but this, all pleasures fancies be.
If ever any beauty I did see,
  Which I desir'd, and got, 'twas but a dream of thee.

And now good morrow to our waking souls,
    Which watch not one another out of fear;
For love, all love of other sights controls,
And makes one little room an everywhere.
Let sea-discoverers to new worlds have gone,
Let maps to other, worlds on worlds have shown,
Let us possess one world, each hath one, and is one.

My face in thine eye, thine in mine appears,
    And true plain hearts do in the faces rest;
Where can we find two better hemispheres,
    Without sharp north, without declining west?
Whatever dies was not mix'd equally;
If our two loves be one, or, thou and I
Love so alike, that none do slacken, none can die.

JOHN DONNE

(1572–1631)

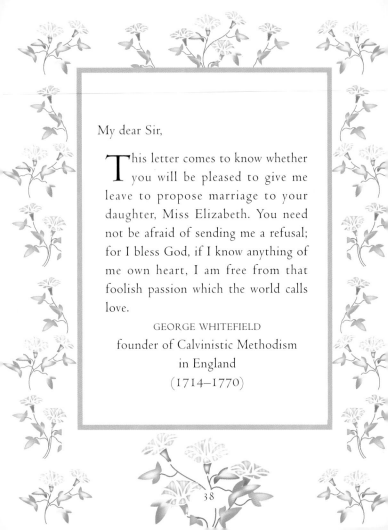

My dear Sir,

This letter comes to know whether you will be pleased to give me leave to propose marriage to your daughter, Miss Elizabeth. You need not be afraid of sending me a refusal; for I bless God, if I know anything of me own heart, I am free from that foolish passion which the world calls love.

GEORGE WHITEFIELD
founder of Calvinistic Methodism
in England
(1714–1770)

There is no more lovely, friendly and charming relationship, communion or company, than a good marriage.

MARTIN LUTHER

(1483–1546)

MARRIAGE

No more alone sleeping, no more alone
    waking,
Thy dreams divided, thy prayers in twain;
Thy merry sisters tonight forsaking,
Never shall we see, maiden, again.

Never shall we see thee, thine eyes
    glancing,
Flashing with laughter and wild in glee,
Under the mistletoe kissing and dancing,
Wantonly free.

There shall come a matron walking sedately,
Low-voiced, gentle, wise in reply.
Tell me, O tell me, can I love her greatly?
All for her sake must the maiden die!

MARY COLERIDGE
(1861–1907)

41

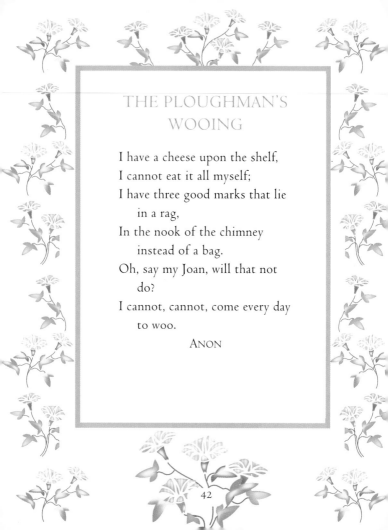

THE PLOUGHMAN'S
WOOING

I have a cheese upon the shelf,
I cannot eat it all myself;
I have three good marks that lie
    in a rag,
In the nook of the chimney
    instead of a bag.
Oh, say my Joan, will that not
    do?
I cannot, cannot, come every day
    to woo.

ANON

Ultimately the bond of all
companionship, whether in marriage or
in friendship, is conversation.

OSCAR WILDE

(1854–1900)

Whereas four young gentlemen, bachelors, in a pretty way of business, capable of rendering any four agreeable young ladies happy, lately disappointed in their amours, are resolved upon a matrimonial state by New Year's Day. If any ladies (Milliners excepted) have a mind to enter the said state, let them enquire at the bar of Grigsby's Coffee House near the Royal Exchange between the hours of four and five for

H.J., B.O., P.J., OR C.J.

Eighteenth-century advertisement

At last you are mine! Soon – in a few months, perhaps, my angel will sleep in my arms, will awaken in my arms, will live there. All your thoughts at all moments, all your looks will be for me; all my thoughts, all my moments, all my looks will be for you!

VICTOR HUGO

(1802–1885)

to his future wife, Adèle Fouchet

Have a heart that never hardens, and a temper that never tires, and a touch that never hurts.

CHARLES DICKENS

(1812–1870)

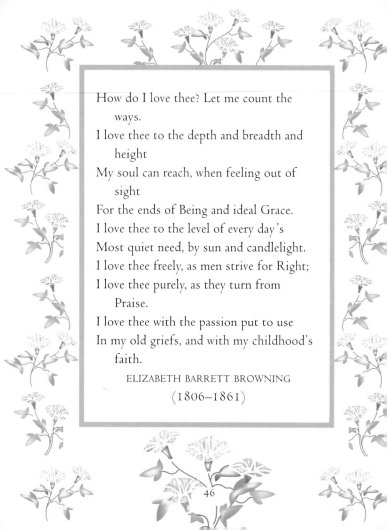

How do I love thee? Let me count the
  ways.
I love thee to the depth and breadth and
  height
My soul can reach, when feeling out of
  sight
For the ends of Being and ideal Grace.
I love thee to the level of every day's
Most quiet need, by sun and candlelight.
I love thee freely, as men strive for Right;
I love thee purely, as they turn from
  Praise.
I love thee with the passion put to use
In my old griefs, and with my childhood's
  faith.

ELIZABETH BARRETT BROWNING

(1806–1861)

Ilove you not only for what you are, but for what I
am when I am with you. I love you not only for
what you have made of yourself, but for what you
are making of me. I love you for the part of me that
you bring out.

ELIZABETH BARRETT BROWNING

(1806–1861)

Ilook back, and in every one point, every word and
gesture, every letter, every silence – you have been
entirely perfect to me – I would not change one word,
one look. My hope and aim are to preserve this love,
not to fall from it ...

ROBERT BROWNING

(1812–1889)

to Elizabeth Barrett, on the day
of their secret marriage

Matrimony should be considered as an incident in life, which, if it comes at all, must come without any contrivance of yours.

A Manual of Etiquette for Ladies

(1855)

Of course, I do have a slight advantage over the rest of you. It helps in a pinch to be able to remind your bride that you gave up a throne for her.

DUKE OF WINDSOR

(1894–1972)

Tears are now bad form. The bride who cries at her wedding is considered to pay her bridegroom a very bad compliment.

MRS HUMPHRY

from *Manners for Women*

(1897)

What greater thing is there for two
human souls than to feel that they are
joined together
to strengthen each other in all labour,
to minister to each other in all sorrow,
to share with each other in all gladness,
to be one with each other in the silent
unspoken memories?

GEORGE ELIOT

(1819–1880)

Whoso findeth a wife, findeth a
good thing.

PROVERBS 18:22

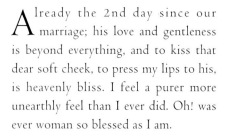

Already the 2nd day since our marriage; his love and gentleness is beyond everything, and to kiss that dear soft cheek, to press my lips to his, is heavenly bliss. I feel a purer more unearthly feel than I ever did. Oh! was ever woman so blessed as I am.

QUEEN VICTORIA
Journal entry
(1840)

Places that are empty of you are empty of all life.

DANTE GABRIEL ROSSETTI
(1828–1882)
to Jane Morris

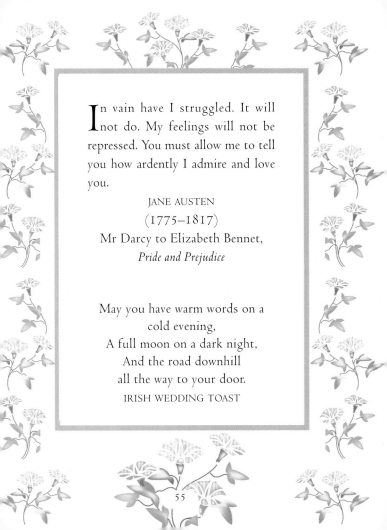

In vain have I struggled. It will not do. My feelings will not be repressed. You must allow me to tell you how ardently I admire and love you.

JANE AUSTEN

(1775–1817)

Mr Darcy to Elizabeth Bennet,
Pride and Prejudice

May you have warm words on a
cold evening,
A full moon on a dark night,
And the road downhill
all the way to your door.

IRISH WEDDING TOAST

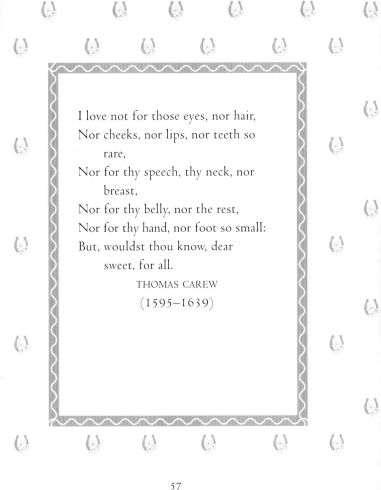

I love not for those eyes, nor hair,
Nor cheeks, nor lips, nor teeth so
    rare,
Nor for thy speech, thy neck, nor
    breast,
Nor for thy belly, nor the rest,
Nor for thy hand, nor foot so small:
But, wouldst thou know, dear
    sweet, for all.

THOMAS CAREW
(1595–1639)

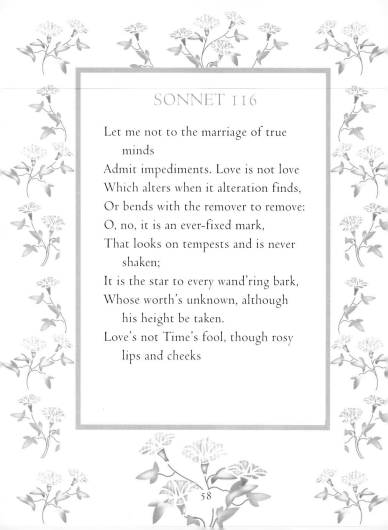

SONNET 116

Let me not to the marriage of true
    minds
Admit impediments. Love is not love
Which alters when it alteration finds,
Or bends with the remover to remove:
O, no, it is an ever-fixed mark,
That looks on tempests and is never
    shaken;
It is the star to every wand'ring bark,
Whose worth's unknown, although
    his height be taken.
Love's not Time's fool, though rosy
    lips and cheeks

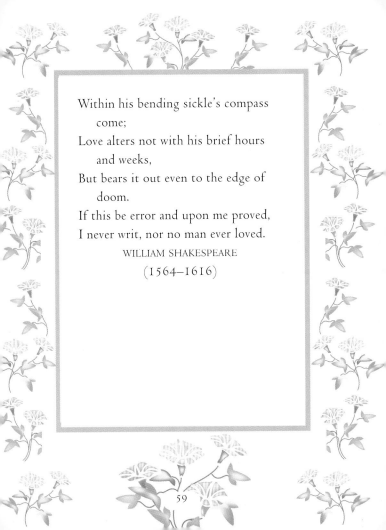

Within his bending sickle's compass
    come;
Love alters not with his brief hours
    and weeks,
But bears it out even to the edge of
    doom.
If this be error and upon me proved,
I never writ, nor no man ever loved.

WILLIAM SHAKESPEARE

(1564–1616)

Good God! how I feel! ... if I am not married in forty-eight hours I am no more ... I am half-dead. Good God! What will become of me? I shall go mad, most undoubtedly!

PRINCE AUGUSTUS, son of George III,
to Lady Augusta Murray
(1793)

I swear I will love thee with my whole heart and think my life well spent if it can make thine happy.

THOMAS CARLYLE, HISTORIAN
(1795–1881)
to his future wife,
Jane Welsh

MY LUVE IS LIKE
A RED,
RED ROSE

My luve is like a red, red rose,
 That's newly sprung in June:
My luve is like the melodie,
 That's sweetly play'd in tune.

As fair art thou, my bonnie lass,
 So deep in luve am I;
And I will luve thee still, my dear,
 Till a' the seas gang dry.

Till a' the seas gang dry, my dear,
  And the rocks melt wi' the sun;
And I will luve thee still, my dear,
  While the sands o' life shall run.

And fare-thee-well, my only luve!
  And fare-thee-well a while!
And I will come again, my luve,
  Tho' 'twere ten thousand mile.

ROBERT BURNS
(1759–1796)

Acknowledgements

Jacket picture, page 3 (detail) and page 47 The Bride from *American Girls in Miniature*, 1912 by Harrison Fisher (1875–1934). Mary Evans Picture Library, 59 Tranquil Vale, Blackheath, London SE3 0BS.

page 8 'Here Comes the Bride', the Wedding of George and Martha Washington in 1759 by Jean Leon Jerome Ferris (1863–1930). Private Collection/Bridgeman Art Library.

page 15 The Bride from *Illustreret Tidende*, 1904 by L. Tuxen (1853–1927). Mary Evans Picture Library, 59 Tranquil Vale, Blackheath, London SE3 0BS.

page 21 A Quaker Wedding by J. Walter West reproduced in *Towards the Light* by Joseph Bibby, early 19th century. Mary Evans Picture Library, 59 Tranquil Vale, Blackheath, London SE3 0BS.

page 23 The Village Wedding by Sir Luke Fildes (1844–1927). Christopher Wood Gallery, London, UK/Bridgeman Art Library.

page 26 The Wedding Morning, 1892 by John Henry Frederick Bacon (1868–1914). Lady Lever Art Gallery, Port Sunlight, Merseyside, UK/Bridgeman Art Library. Trustees of the National Museums & Galleries on Merseyside.

page 31 Signing the Register by Edmund Blair Leighton (1853–1922). Bristol City Museum and Art Gallery, UK/Bridgeman Art Library.

page 37 The Wedding Ceremony from *American Girls in Miniature*,1912 by Harrison Fisher (1875–1934). Mary Evans Picture Library, 59 Tranquil Vale, Blackheath, London SE3 0BS.

page 43 The Wedding Meal at Yport by Albert-Auguste Fourie (b. 1854). Musée des Beaux-Arts, Rouen, France/Bridgeman Art Library/Lauros/Giraudon/Bridgeman Art Library.

page 49 Conversation in a Park, portrait of the artist and his wife, Margaret Burr (1728–98) at the time of their marriage, 1746 by Thomas Gainsborough (1727–88). Louvre, Paris, France/Bridgeman Art Library, credit: Peter Willi.

page 50 Engaged! and with a Ring to Prove it! by Will Grete, reproduced in *The Printing Art* c. 1913. Mary Evans Picture Library, 59 Tranquil Vale, Blackheath, London SE3 0BS.

page 52 The Bride Cuts the Cake at a Smart Wedding Party by an unnamed artist in the *Girl's Own Paper*, 2 October 1897. Mary Evans Picture Library, 59 Tranquil Vale, Blackheath, London SE3 0BS.

All other pictures are from a private collection.